IBERIAN RAILS:
LAST DAYS OF THE OLD ORDER

The railways of Spain and Portugal on the eve of modernization

VOLUME 2:
Valencia, Grenada, Meseta

By Fred Matthews

Gotham Books

30 N Gould St.
Ste. 20820, Sheridan, WY 82801
https://gothambooksinc.com/

Phone: 1 (307) 464-7800

© 2023 *Fred Matthews.* All rights reserved.

No part of this book may be reproduced, stored in a retrieval system, or transmitted by any means without the written permission of the author.

Published by Gotham Books (December 27, 2023)

ISBN: 979-8-88775-717-9 (H)
ISBN: 979-8-88775-715-5 (P)
ISBN: 979-8-88775-716-2 (E)

Because of the dynamic nature of the Internet, any web addresses or links contained in this book may have changed since publication and may no longer be valid.

The views expressed in this work are solely those of the author and do not necessarily reflect the views of the publisher, and the publisher hereby disclaims any responsibility for them.

This book is dedicated to the memory of
Laurence Russ Veysey 1932 – 2004
Great Scholar
Passionate Rail Enthusiast
Stormy Petrel

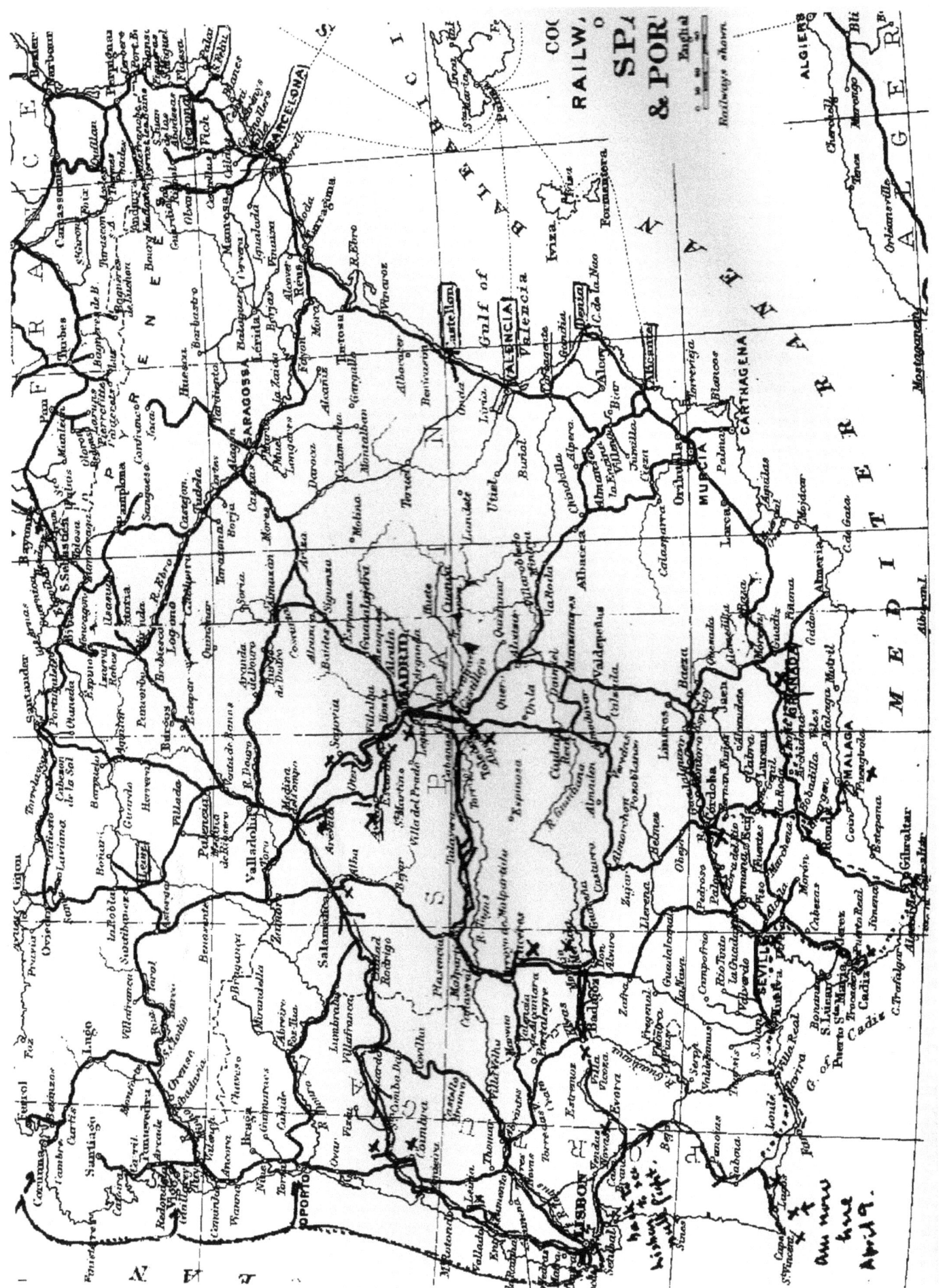

RENFE action at Castellon de la Plana: a German-built 4-6-0 of 1913, the standard Norte passenger engine until the late 1920s, pulls the 12.10 PM local to Valencia past heavy dual-service 4-8-0 #2261, one of hundreds built in the 1920s for the old Madrid Zaragoza & Alicante by Maquinista in Barcelona.

INTRODUCTION

This is the second volume of a survey of Iberian railways and tramways in 1963, when my old friend Larry Veysey and I made a long circular tour of the Peninsula. In 1963 the traditional tramways, at least in Spain, were large and busy, though already in the sights of modernizing bureaucrats. The broad-gauge national RENFE and most independent railways were still largely powered by steam; many passengers rode in wood-bodied coaches. Much of the railway scene was comparable to that of North America around 1910. Volume I covered the railways and tramways of Catalonia. Here we make a loop south along the Mediterranean Coast to Valencia and Alicante, inland to Granada, and north via Madrid and León to the Costa Verde along the Bay of Biscay.

The RENFE (Red National des Ferrocariles Españoles) is a government-owned system created in 1941 to consolidate four major and some minor broad-gauge companies left without reconstruction funds at the end of the bloody, destructive Civil War in 1939. Despite inheriting a broken and bankrupt group of companies, RENFE had little new funding until the late 1940s, except for necessary repairs and replacements. Spain was struggling with savage domestic repression, then ostracism and isolation by the victorious democratic powers after Generalissimo Franco's Axis friends were finally defeated in 1945.

When money for improvement began to flow again, it went first to new steam power, mostly home-built. Spain, like Britain, had vast coal deposits (often low-grade) but relatively little domestic oil. It also faced a persistent lack of foreign exchange, due partly to Franco's hostility to foreign influences, including capital. Hence, new home-built steam, until external relations improved in the mid-50s as the United States saw Spain as a reliable ally against Communism. Even then, given the masses of skilled, low-paid steam men, construction of steam continued until after US aid (often in kind) and new economic advisors led to a policy of dieselization from 1958.

The first flower of postwar re-equipping were 342 heavy 2-8-2s, of class 141/2101, built between 1953 and 1960 by North British and (mostly) the four major Spanish builders, Macosa, Maquinista, Eskalduna, and Babcock & Wilcox. Although numerous, the big Mikados were not typical of RENFE motive power—they were some 15% of the 3000-plus steam locos, more than balanced by several hundred ancient teakettles built before 1890. Most of these senior citizens were 0-6-0s or 0-8-0s, built as road engines but now serving modest days on not-very-busy local switching duties. You could, however, still see them around Valencia on medium-distance local passenger and mixed trains. RENFE's most numerous types were some 680 big 4-8-0s of various designs, built with government aid during the 1920s. There were also over 500 2-8-0s, and over 200 each of 0-6-0s, 4-6-0s, 0-8-0s, 2-8-2s and 4-8-2s, plus a variety of other types including tank engines and a few Beyer-Garratts and compound Mallets.

The best English-language introductions to Spanish railways in the 1960s are L.G. Marshall's *Steam on the RENFE* (Macmillan, 1965) and two books by D. Trevor Rowe: *Railway Holiday in Spain* (David & Charles, 1966); *and Spain and Portugal* (Continental Railway Handbook, Ian Allan, 1970). Rowe gave some basic statistics for the broad-gauge RENFE system which was decreed in 1941 and operational from 1943. The RENFE had about 7126 route-miles, along with extensive unfinished sections that had been delayed, often destroyed, by the bitter Civil War. By the late 1960s, route-mileage had risen to 8563, as several long lines were completed: Zamora-Ourense, Madrid-Burgos "direct," Cuenca-Valencia. In the 1940s, much of the (re)construction work on these routes was done by convict labor–political prisoners, supporters of the defeated Republic, whose mortality rate was considerable. Track on main lines had improved, but there were still thousands of miles of light, jointed rail.

Steam was still the dominant motive power in the early 1960s, with over 3000, but diesels were arriving in substantial numbers, so that by late 1968 there were 700 active steam locos, all now oil-burning, as against about 650 full-sized diesels and some 20 TALGO locos. Electrification had been expanding slowly for decades; by 1968 there were about 360 electric locos running over 1900 route-miles.

Passenger rolling-stock was beginning to be standardized with modern double-truck metal-bodied cars. At the end of 1963 there were 1462 wood-bodied coaches (some of the double truck ones fairly new and comfortable) and 954 modern metal cars. Over 900 four-wheel coaches ran in 1949; 316 in 1967. Completing the roster were automotors–diesel or gasoline railcars. About 30 railcars, turned out in brilliant silver, dated from 1935-41, and Fiat had supplied fifty 3-car TAF (Tren Automotor Fiat) sets from 1952 for daytime express service. The low-slung, ultra-lightweight Talgo, the great Spanish contribution to modern railroading, was about to emerge from infancy; but in 1963 only a couple ran Madrid-Irun and Madrid-Barcelona expresses, less than daily.

The presence of numerous independent narrow-gauge railways resulted from Spain's tangled and troubled railway history. The broad-gauge main lines began first, from the 1840s, with major construction financed by foreign capital between 1850 and 1880. The broad gauge was probably chosen for military reasons, to make invasion from Europe more difficult. In the 1840s two major invasions, by NapoLeón and then by the restored French monarchy in 1822-3, to crush a liberal government, were still within living memory. The choice may have made a major difference a century later--legend has it that in 1940-41 Hitler had planned to send an army across Spain to capture Gibraltar, until his generals warned that the break of gauge at the French border was a major problem.

Spanish narrow gauges came a generation or more after the broad, as local and foreign interests agitated for cheaper ways to connect towns and exploit natural resources. Away from the few large cities and rich huerta (irrigated plain) along the Mediterranean coast, there was an impoverished traditional society, with poor roads, few canals, and difficult transport. The early broad-gauge system, like the earlier royal roads, was largely a hub-and-spoke network focused on Madrid, still reflecting the

Hapsburg monarchy's drive to create a centralized nation out of several regional societies. Much of the land, therefore, was without railways, though often with rich resources waiting for exploitation, and always with local elites convinced that a railway would be their lifeline to prosperity. But capital (mostly foreign) was cautious, except where (as in Asturias and at the great Rio Tinto complex in Andalucia) foreign corporations created little enclaves of their own, to mine for export.

In this endemic state of capital starvation, anything that could cut costs substantially was a godsend, and a sizeable literature extolling the narrow gauge appeared (as in the U.S. at the same time). Between 1870 and 1910 a series of laws gave, or permitted, state and regional subsidies to "secondary" and "strategic" railways, the latter a way to justify subsidies in the name of national defense.

At first most of these secondary lines were meter-gauge, but as costs even there proved daunting, in the 1880s a new campaign began for ultra-narrow gauge, 75 cm (¾ meter, or 2'5½") gauge. These unstable-looking "toy trains" proved surprisingly successful and long-lived; but their slow speeds created severe vulnerability once roads improved.

Originally, most of the narrow-gauge lines were privately operated, though often with local government participation. As road traffic began to bite them, as early as 1930 in some areas, those considered still useful were taken over, or subsidized, by government, and called Estado lines, though still using their old names. As weaker lines closed, equipment was shifted around. There were still several major private narrow-gauge lines in 1963, notably along and inland from the Bay of Biscay in the north, where industry was heavy and thick. After the mid-sixties, government limitation on rates led to losses, and then to either closure or takeover by the new government narrow-gauge company directorate known as FEVE (Ferrocariles de Via Estrecha).

El Parderole: little number 7 of the FC de Onda al Grao de Castellan, a 75 cm (2'5½") gauge 0-6-2 tank, built by Krauss in 1890 and rebuilt by the company in 1960, creeps through Castellón's centre with a train from Onda.

Meeting the competition: Onda–Castellón 6, another Krauss 0-6-2T, crosses ahead. of the new suburban trolley coach line

Out to the Grao: little "cockroach" No.5 with hundreds of bathers heads out of Castellón on the three-mile run to the harbor.

CHAPTER I

RAILS OF THE *HUERTA*: CASTELLON, VALENCIA, GANDIA

After a few days savoring Barcelona's trams, buildings, and interurbans, we boarded the overnight Valencia sleeper, south to a dawn arrival at Castellón to begin exploring the rail empire of the huerta, Spain's "golden fringe," the rich irrigated coastal plain that lines the Mediterranean from below Tortosa to south of Murcia (with a mountainous intrusion below Valencia). The huerta, cultivated and irrigated since Moorish times a thousand years ago, grew a half-dozen crops for domestic use and export, largely by coastwise shipping even after the broad-gauge railway arrived around 1860. Grains and rice were grown, but the region's prosperity rested on intensely-cultivated fields of apricots, date palms, mulberry, and above all orange groves.

The productivity and prosperity of this "fruit garden of Spain" stimulated the growth of cities, and a need for branch line railways to bring crops from plain to town and harbor for transfer point. Given the Madrid-orientation and capital shortage of the broad-gauge companies, a number of these were narrow-gauge shortlines. Our overnight sleeper brought us to the first, and arguably the most enjoyable, of these little lines as it puffed into Castellón de la Plana (now Castelló) at 6.15 on a Sunday morning.

Castellón, four miles inland from its port, was a sizeable city, with about 55,000 inhabitants in 1950. It was not a tourist town, having been heavily damaged in the Civil War. But it had been rebuilt in neo-traditional style, with narrow streets lined by tall apartments. And through these streets ran the tiny 75cm steam trains of the FC de Onda al Grao de Castellón. The O-C had opened to the Grao (landing place) in 1888, and through the city and out to Onda in 1890. It ran several trains a day through city streets and then roadside to Onda, and a separate service from the station, also roadside to the port. On weekends this was a busy operation: despite a competing rural trolley coach line and informal bus and truck jitneys, two trains were operating, running a rough half-hour service, extended at the Grao over little-used freight spurs to a point near the beaches. With its tiny 0-6-0 and 0-6-2 tanks built by Krauss in 1888-90 (plus two newer tanks from an abandoned line at Gerona), the Onda Castellón was the ultimate charmer in steam: according to Peter Allen and Robert Wheeler in Steam on the Sierra, locals called it *El Parderole*, "a kind of cockroach," which fit well with its motion over the very light rail.

And *El Parderole* looked to be thriving, with crowded little trains shuttling to the beach. In fact, it closed about six weeks later. It had been Estado-run for decades; there was little freight traffic left, and buses, 'collectivo' passenger-hauling trucks, and the motor bikes that plagued our photography, were considered sufficient replacement once the rail seemed exhausted. We were lucky not to have delayed our trip.

Around noon, after a hasty snack, we watched heavy mainline action at the RENFE depot. We found a long, indeed an American-length, freight in the siding, headed by one of the numerous heavy 4-8-0s, built in the 1920s, when the Primo de Rivera government gave subsidies to purchase new equipment. Soon a German-built 4-6-0 of 1913 accelerated from the station on a Valencia local. A few minutes later, the earth shook as the big 4-8-0 made like the Santa Fe as it moved its solid train of refrigerator cars out. We caught another "omnibus" second/third class train to Valencia an hour later.

Which stimulated some reflections on Spain's passenger services. Having the luxury of a second train an hour later was a rarity in the Spain of 1963, when main lines beyond the suburbs were characterized by services both slow and infrequent. The Valencian huerta was more prosperous and populous than inland Spain, so could support a heavy passenger service by Spanish standards. There were four through trains from Barcelona, including the customary mid-afternoon TAF railcar, which took six hours for about 228 miles with fifteen intermediate stops. Earlier, at 11 AM, Spain's longest run, the Barcelona-Seville Rapido, headed south, taking 8½ hours with 26 stops to Valencia (and another 15 ¼ hours to cover the 475 miles on to Seville). This train was a target for railfans, since from Tarragona, where the Barcelona electric zone ended, it usually drew one of Europe's only long, lanky Beyer-Garratt locomotives in passenger service. There were also several local trains at each end of the route, five of them from Castellón to Valencia.

Maquinista-built 240-2261 restarts its train at Castellón, following a local passenger. The long train was composed of empty Transfesa refrigerator cars returning from Europe, after having their wheels exchanged at the border. Transfesa was an early, and successful, effort to compete with trucks and coastwise shipping for the lucrative trade in Valencian produce.

Duty done: the stationmaster carries his rolled red flag back to the station after giving the all-clear to the next station to Train 702, the 11-car Seville-Barcelona Rapido. #702 had departed Seville at 6.45 last evening and today will likely reach Barcelona around 8.30PM

Modern engine, ancient background: the pre-Roman fortress at Sagunto, on the Peves de Pajarito, with a 1950s 2-8-2 running light on the old Central of Aragon line, which paralleled the former Norte main from here into Valencia

This was lavish service by Spanish standards, and a considerable improvement of the service in 1900, when Baedeker complained of average speeds of 18 miles per hour. Even by 1963 speeds were well above the 1900 average. On a stretch south of Castellón, two Rapidos averaged about 30 mph between stops, and the TAF over 40 mph over the same 19 miles. On the Madrid-Zaragoza main line, with its new rail, the superfast TALGO took 250 minutes for 214 miles, or over 50 mph nonstop; the TAF close to 50 mph, and two Rapidos around 40 mph.

Out on the central tableland, the meseta, the typical pattern of service was a "fast" afternoon railcar, often only three per week, an overnight express with sleeping cars, and a mid-morning semi-fast. Sometimes this served as the all-stop Correo; sometimes the Correo ran separately. So there were at most four daily trains on "heavy" days, (usually two or three, since the morning express often alternated with the TAF), plus a few locals around larger cities.

Various explanations can be offered for the RENFE's spartan service. Away from the coast, and Madrid, Spain was not thickly populated, and most people were still poor. Government attitudes may have played a role; the railways were not high priority until later, indeed to a degree until after 1990, and their slow schedules put them at a disadvantage as roads were improved. Perhaps long-distance travel was not a priority for a government that had told Spaniards they must work hard at low wages to expiate the sin of supporting an anti-Christian government in the 1930s. Long-distance travel was for the political and economic elite, who were likely to use airplanes or overnight sleepers. There remains RENFE's stringent bureaucratic system of controlling longer-distance travel, which suggests that demand was already present. Most longer-distance trains required reservations which required waiting at the right window at the right time and then waiting again on the day of the journey to have the ticket validated. The hours and location, of both were variable; sometimes the window for validating the ticket would close 10-15 minutes before departure. These procedures were justified by the shortage of cars fit for longer trips, but perhaps they were also a means of controlling the mobility of an increasingly restive people. Spain's tradition of authoritarian control didn't begin with Franco; it dated back at least 350 years to Philip II. Perhaps the RENFE could be seen as part of the vast system by which the austere, bureaucratic Castilians controlled their more volatile and entrepreneurial neighbors around the coasts.

My reflection on these issues was suddenly interrupted, after we took siding a few stations below Castellón. After a few minutes an odd sound grew and the amazing sight appeared of the Seville-Barcelona Rapido, running over an hour late, with about ten fairly modern, mostly-wood-bodied cars. On the point was a high-drivered Beyer-Garratt built in 1930 for the Central Aragon line. After a long, active morning, I had been off-guard, not realizing that we hadn't crossed this legendary train.

Below Sagunto, with its ruined pre-Roman fortress, we raced a 2-8-2 running light on the parallel Central of Aragon line, then made the wide sweep to the left around the center of Valencia, to pull into the busy train shed of Valencia Termino (earlier, and later, called Valencia Norte). With its substantial local services and through trains on four routes, this was a very busy place, with some hundred arrivals and departures per day. Most of all, it was still largely a steam-powered station, with at least three quarters of those trains pulled by a wide variety of locos, from eighty-year-old 0-6-0s through 1910-era 4-6-0s and 0-6-6-0s, to the heavy 4-8-0s of circa 1925, the 1950s 2-8-2s, and 4-6-2/2-6-4 passenger Garratts of 1930. To complete the dream scene, there was still a footbridge across the station throat, ideal for photography which seems to have been tolerated by the local police.

The busy engine terminal near Valencia Termino (now Norte) station, with a 462/0401 class passenger Garratt and a couple of 0-6-0s visible.

Inside Valencia Termino: an MZA 4-8-0, a Fiat TAF, and anxious passengers.

One of the named 030/2067 class engines built by Hartmann in Chemnitz, Germany, in 1882-85, with an arrived local train and one of its contingents of Civil Guards (two or three of whom rode every train).

The Villalba, the first of the Hartmann 0-6-0s of 1882, on an omnibus for the short branch to Liria.

One of the German 4-6-0s of c. 1909 backing a train of modern steel cars (with traditional wood seats) into Valencia Termino.

A 462/0401 class passenger Garratt brings the heavy Barcelona-Seville express into Valencia. These six engines were built in 1930 for the heavily- graded Central of Aragon (Valencia-Zaragoza) by Eskalduna in Bilbao, and were the heaviest locos in Spain until the 2-10-28 and 4-8-4s of the 1950s. With 69" drivers (compared to 47" on the freight Garratts) they were fast as well as powerful, and spent their last decade assigned to Valencia, especially on the Barcelona-Seville Rapido. In the background, one of the silver Hungarian railcars of 1935-37.

The passenger Garratt crosses to the east side of the station, with the Barcellona-Seville Rapido, Train 701. It will have a half-hour here for servicing and a new locomotive. Seville is 15 hours ahead.

The junction station at Pl. del Caudillo, on the Valencia tramway system.

Neo-baroque City (and trams): the plaza del caudillo (now Ayuntamiento) looking south at the huge Valencia Termino trainshed.

Routes joining: a bit north of the Pl. Caudillo, two lines met before the 18th Century belfry of the Iglesia de Santa Caterina.

Not quite as old as the Migualete, the cathedral tower of 1280-1360, Valencia's traditional symbol. A lineup of c. 1910-1915 cars at the Plaza de la Reina, heading for Caudillo.

Given this star attraction, plus some meter-gauge steam to the south, I saw little of Valencia's busy, traditional meter-gauge tramway. And even less of the ancient city centre of this bustling metropolis, Spain's third-largest (population 503,000 in 1950). Even the giant cathedral, the Séo, with its unique Migualete or octagonal bell-tower, passed with a couple of quick photos.

On a much larger scale, Valencia's tramway was like Mataró's: it was built, converted to electric operation between 1900 and 1915, then ran largely without change (some cars were rebuilt for one-man operation) until the late 1960s. In 1960, according to J. Morley and R. Plant in <u>Minor Railways and Tramways of Eastern Spain</u>, 181 motor and 86 trailer cars ran over about 50 route miles. Morley and Plant imply that this dense traditional system existed because the private Compania de Tranvias Ferrocarriles de Valencia had no money to buy new buses; its franchise would run out in 1967, when the city planned to take over and buy buses. Legend has it that the Valencian trams starred in the epic film <u>Doctor Zhivago</u>, which appeared in 1965, with artificial snow used to simulate Petrograd.

Valencia Termino was endlessly fascinating, but we were also tempted by the meter-gauge railways in the huerta south of the city. We took a morning local train to Carcagente, a town of about 18,000, 24 miles south of the Levante's metropolis. "The cradle of the oranges" was still in the flat plain, surrounded by orange groves; strawberries, olives and mulberries for silk-making were in the hinterland and along the meter-gauge FC Carcagente a Denia, which headed southeast 42 miles, out on the mountainous extrusion into the Mediteranean that ended at Cap Nao.

The Carcagente line was Spain's pioneer narrow gauge, opened in 1864, with horse traction, as far as Gandia (home of the Borgia clan), to bring crops to the newly-opened broad gauge at Carcagente. Steam power, and the extension to Denia involving heavier construction, came in 1881-84. As of 1963 most passenger trips were by automotor, including some tiny vintage cars, but there was at least one Correo, behind shiny Belgian tank engines of 1911-24, and still some freight traffic, including oil for a cement plant in Gandia that came off the connecting coastal meter-gauge at Denia. The C-D's route was a mix of rich green fields—"the richest and most populous huerta of the Kingdom of Valencia," said Baedeker in 1901—with brisk climbs over spurs of the mountains that crowded the plain into ever-narrower strips.

At Gandia, a bit over half way along, the C-D crossed and joined a different kind of meter-gauge railway, the Alcoy and Gandia Railway and Harbour Company. The A & G was built and operated by an English company with interests in the paper and textile mills of Alcoy, an industrial city of some 50,000, located along a rushing river up in the mountains about 35 miles south of Gandia. Like several foreign-operated companies, the A-G moved fuel up from the harbor and finished goods out, part of a trade-chain independent of the RENFE. At Alcoy, the A-G met another, larger, company, the 63-mile FC Economicos de Vilena a Alcoy y Yecla, making Gandia the hub of a major narrow gauge empire.

But the A-G was not flourishing. As Morley and Plant put it: "the Company has been in financial difficulties for many years, and receives an annual subsidy from the state, no balance sheet having been issued since 1935. It has not been taken over by the Estado as agreement has not yet been reached over realistic compensation." Clearly, within a few years, alternative shipping patterns removed the need for the A-G.

The Alcoy & Gandia was said to be a beautiful line, winding up sheer rock gorges into the dry mountains, but the slow trains and sparse schedule limited us to snapping pictures of the line's classic Beyer-Peacock 2-6-2 tanks of 1890-91, all named, in sequence, for towns along the line, Gandia to Alcoy. The weather was a bit smoggy, even in 1963, from nearby industry, but opportunities were provided by the elaborate backing-and-switching operation by which trains to and from the Puerto came into the Gandia station, next to the C-D's. The huerta was rich in railways as well as produce.

One of the original engines of the FC. Carcagente a Denia in the huerta south of Valencia. These little saddle-tanks came in 1881-3 from Black Hawthorn of Gateshead, England.

C-D's 12.15 train to Denia was a tiny ferro bus, dateless in the sources but looking comfortably pre-1950. At Carcagente, with the RENFE line behind.

At Gandia, our Ferrobus meets an FC Carcagente-Denia freight behind Estado 27, a Belgian 0-6-0T of 1924.

Gandia at Gandia. The PC Alcoy à Puerta de Gandia's Number One, built by Beyer Peacock in Manchester in 1890, prepares to depart for Alcoy, up in the mountains just visible, with train 3, the 1.15 PM Correo.

Alcoy-Gandia's Gandia backing out of town onto its own line to the east. Six of the original eight of these charmers survived for almost 80 years until the line was closed by its Estado subsidizers.

Nearing Denia: at Vergel, we meet the Carcagente-Denia's westbound Coreo behind another of the Belgian 0-6-0Ts. Denia's signature mountain, the Mongo, looms ahead

CHAPTER II

BRILLIANT LIGHT AND STEAM: ALICANTE AND THE COSTA BLANCA

Thus far, on our leisurely journey south along Spain's Mediterranean coast, we had had to look from a distance at the mountains that shadowed the huerta to the west. Finally, moving on to Alicante on the 9 AM Rapido with portions for Madrid via Albacete, and for Alicante, we charged them head-on. Since the Castilian mountains flowed out to the sea below Jativa (30 miles south of Valencia), railway-builders had two choices: to skirt the mountains out around Cape Nao via Denia, as connecting narrow gauge lines did, or to tackle the mountains, as RENFE's main Valencia-Madrid line did.

Our 9 AM Rapido, behind a pair of powerful 4-8-0s, built for the MZA, had a Madrid portion behind the engines, and behind a furgone (baggage-caboose with recessed ends), our Alicante cars. We were nine cars away from the noisy power, but sound and smoke were powerfully present on the rear vestibule of the last coach. Beyond Jativa began the climb away from the huerta into arid terrain still dotted with olive groves. As Baedeker said, "the sudden transition from the sub-tropical luxuriance of Valencia to these cold steppes is very striking in winter." It was summer, and we braved wind and soot to record a sidetracked downhill freight, behind a 2-8-2+2-8-2 freight Garratt and a 4-8-0, as we blasted up towards Mogente.

Beyond a long tunnel under the Montana de Marioga came the junction at La Encina, where our section was cut off and taken down the rocky valley of the Vinalapó River, past ruined castles perched on rocks, onto the huerta around Alicante. We had taken 5½ hours for 112 miles; the coastal narrow gauges would have required several hours longer. As we swung around to the south to reach the rather quiet Alicante Termino, a rare bonus appeared–the shed pilot (shop switcher) 020/0233, a tiny teakettle built by Couillet, Belgium, in 1885, pulling a shuttle from the station to the loco shed.

Like the American southwest 30 years earlier: climbing away from Jativa, the double-headed 0900 express from Valencia to Madrid and Alicante blasts up towards the Montana de Mariaga.

In the hole: a class 282 freight Garratt, a 4-8-0 behind, wait in siding above Mogente, with a long train of tank cars, for our southbound express to clear. The Garratt was one of sixteen, a half dozen built for the Central Aragon in 1930, the other ten by the same builder, Babcock & Wilcox in Bilbao, in 1961 as one of RENFE's final steam orders.

"Whistle." Now climbing close to the summit tunnel, Train 501, with its pair of 4-5-0s, looks very Southern Pacific.

The town of Sax, 18 miles beyond the junction of La Encina, as the train drops down the Vinalapó river towards Alicante.

Rare bird: a 78-year-old 0-4-0 tank engine (Couillet, Belgium, 1885) with the workers' shuttle between Alicante Termino station and the engine shed. Alicante's bare castle-rock, the Castillo de Santa Barbara, in the background.

Our home for the next few days now calls itself "Alicant," in the Valencian tongue; in 1963, under Franco, it was "Alicante," in Castilian. Alicante, according to Michelin's Spain "has always been enjoyed for its remarkable, luminous skies." Known as "the white citadel" to the Greeks and "city of light" to the Romans, it had still been a compact city of 50,000 in 1900, too small in size to have a tram system until around 1920. The railways began to bring holidaymakers by 1900; by 1950, with a population of 101,000, it was emerging as a major resort, the capital of the fast-growing Costa Blanca along the white coast to the northeast. Northern Europeans were beginning to arrive by plane. Alicante itself was largely early-20th century, with sprawling low-density suburbs.

Alicante's tramway system comprised seven routes over 32 route-km, including a good deal of duplication, all single- track including loops, some out into the village-like suburbs. 41 little four-wheel cars and 21 similar trailers, most built in the early 1920s, provided service. This was another typical Spanish tramway, built by the private Tramvias y Electricidad in the early 1920s, taken over by the municipality in 1957 when the franchise expired, and operated for about another decade until buses were affordable.

For me the chief attraction of Alicante, along with its warmth and clear light, was what has become a truly splendid survivor, the scenic meter-gauge E.S.A. line that wanders up the Costa Blanca some 55 miles through the burgeoning resort zone and on past unchanged white villages to the little port of Denia beyond Cape Nao. Built quite late, as two separate companies, a "secondary" north from Alicante and "strategic" for the remainder to Denia, it opened in 1914-15, worked as one line, the Estregico de Alicante. Its remarkable survival into the 21st century is probably due to the difficulty of building wide roads in the dense area of high-rise vacation apartments already building as far northeast as Benidorm.

Denia, the E.S.A's terminus and connecting-point for the line for Carcagente, was ancient–a Phoenician settlement, then Roman, then Moorish. Its vast ruined castle above the town was said to date back to Moorish if not Roman times, but was active as late as 1813, when it was the last NapoLeónic fortress in Spain, defending a five-month siege before surrendering. The area around Denia and Cape Nao was a major location in Patrick O'Brian's novel Master and Commander, set around 1800 when the coastwise trade, essential due to the lack of roads, was disrupted by pirates and British commerce-raiders. Perhaps the E.S.A. really was strategic.

In 1963 the E.S.A. ran several Benidorm trains, but a sparse service beyond–three or four railcars plus the high point of the day, a steam- powered mixed train that went north in the morning, simmered in Denia during the hottest hours, then made a truly enchanting journey through the rich late light along the romantic white coast, past the mini-Gibraltar of the Penyal de Ifuch and the white villages. We paused to switch en route, allowing many photo-opps. The pair of tricorned-hatted Guardias Civiles chatted good-naturedly with the passengers, and looked away when they saw me produce a camera. (With two exceptions this was the rule in Spain; only once, at Madrid Atocha with an angry employee, not a policeman, was there a tense encounter).

The E.S.A. had a couple of charming 4-wheel railcars home-built in 1949 for short runs, and the standard Swiss-style, Spanish-built Estado railcars of 1958. The steam train drew one of ten "plain, tubby, Germanic 2-6-0 tanks" built in 1913 by Honomag or La Maquinista in Barcelona to the same design. As Allen and Wheeler complained, if only this beautiful line had had the lovely Beyer Peacocks from the Alcoy-Gandia! The E.S.A. still had freight in 1963, trains of fuel from Alicante Puerto to the Gandia cement works. The 1973 Cook's Continental showed a through passenger service from Alicante to Gandia, now run by the province. Presumably the freight traffic preserved the Denia-Gandia. Now Alicante-Denia thrives, and a RENFE broad-gauge line from Valencia reaches Gandia along the coast. Despite all the new concrete block apartments, the Costa Blanca's meter-gauge line remains a starred destination.

A small system: car One of Alicante's Servicio Municipal de Tranvias making its downtown loop on Route 2 to Carolinas, with the harbor in the distance.

Cars of three routes heading through downtown Alicante en route to single-track lines through bright, dusty suburbs. The yellow cars were supplied from abroad when the system opened in 1924.

Urban Spain, 1963-a representative view, in this case on Alicante Route 2 to Carolinas.

Alicante's Carolinas line on the southwestern fringe, with Mount Benacantil looming above the center.

Beach railway: the sunbathers are out as ESA's 10-spot, built in 1913 by Maquinista of Barcelona to a German design, makes up the morning mixed train to Denia

Little Giant: ESA assembled two tiny Ferrobuses in its own shops in 1949-50, the era of make-do-and-mend. They could haul trailers.

Ready to depart Denia, with the Mongó looming. ESA had 28 coaches and 4 furgones (combines) in 1959, all built in the 1910s for the line's opening.

Way station: adding pickup freight soon after leaving Denia.

Circling in and out beneath the coastal mountains as ESA's afternoon mixed approaches Altea

ESA's German-designed Maquinista tank engine taking water at Altea, with the medieval town on the hillside above the station.

Chapter III

DEEP SOUTH: VICTORIAN RAILWAY TO GRANADA

From Alicante, we had the chance to experience Spanish rail travel as it had been in 1910. The secondary route to Granada had been pieced together from a group of small private companies built for other purposes, which remained separate until RENFE absorbed them in 1941. The mines that had inspired some had mostly run out, so they had been in financial trouble for years, and RENFE saw little value in upgrading a useful but unprofitable connector. Indeed, this would become the only RENFE through route to be abandoned, south of Almendricos, in the 1980s. The few through passengers would travel back from Alicante to La Encina to catch the Barcelona-Seville express and change at Linares for Granada.

The 258-mile route from Alicante to Granada traversed the (mostly) light rails of four former private companies: the Andaluces to Murcia; then briefly the Madrid Zaragoza & Alicante's Madrid line to Alcantarilla; then the tiny Alcantarilla-Lorca. From Lorca to Baza had been the most celebrated of these lines, the Great Southern Railway of Spain, a British-financed and operated line from the port of Aguilas inland to tap mines in the dry hills that encroached on the huerta. From 1889, for some 75 years, the Great Southern was run almost entirely by one class of locomotive, the 25 2-6-0s that became RENFE's 130/2121 class. These were built by four British builders from 1889 to 1905, and carried Victorian headlights and the names of places along the line. Each engine had a large round builder's plate, in English. With the train of vintage wooden coaches that made up the 6.10 Correo from Alicante to Granada, train 685 (later 885, then 884) they embodied Spanish railroading of about 1910.

The schedule, too, was reminiscent of Baedeker's 1901 average of 18 miles per hour. We were timetabled to make the 258 miles in 15 ¾ hours, with 37 regular and four conditional stops. On the day, we required another 90 minutes. There were two or three engine changes, though one of the old Great Southern Moguls took us out of Alicante.

There is an informative discussion of the GSS in D. Trevor Rowe's Railway Holiday in Spain. It was slightly profitable early in the century, but not after 1920; already before RENFE it had been merged with its southern neighbor, the Baza-Guadix. For better or worse, it may have played a monumental cultural role- legend has it that the British staff of the G.S.S. introduced football to Spain.

The irrigated huerta, in narrowing strips, extended along the line down to near Almendricos, junction for Aguilas and the old Great Southern shops. Beyond came ever-drier rocky hills, some dotted with little villages clustered around ancient Moorish castles. This had been an area of bitter battles between Christian and Muslims during the Reconquista by Christian crusaders, the terrain somewhat resembled California's Owens Valley, home of another fabled railway, but the Owens was wider and flatter. After the Huerta vanished, we labored along the dry canyon of the Rio Almanzora, traversing short tunnels and then climbing arid hills.

Trevor Rowe's Railway Holiday in Spain gives a vivid account of a ride with the driver of the Granada-Valencia *Automotor*, rolling over the bumpy rail around rocky curves: "there are a few short tunnels along here, and the driver hoots loudly and switches on the headlight for even the shortest of these. 'It's not that hitting a peasant or two would do us any harm,' he confides, 'but sometimes they have their donkeys with them!"

From Baza we had a more powerful Andaluces 4-8-0 of 1920, a lanky beast designed for light rail. In the late light at Zujar-Freilà, south of Baja, we took siding. Most passengers alighted to stretch their legs, as we awaited the "fast" of the day, the *Automotor*, train 555/586/556, 8.30 AM from Valencia, scheduled Alicante-Granada in only 9 hours 13 minutes for the 258 miles. The silver bullet soon appeared and rolled cautiously through, sounding its horn, as the stationmaster displayed his rolled flag for the all-clear. This train too was "vintage" even in 1963, a very long Hungarian railcar built in 1937.

It's still early at Alqueiras, some 40 miles and 130 minutes south of Alicante, as Lumbreras and the 6.10.AM Correo to Granada pause to exchange mail. These 1889-style 2-6-0s, built in Glasgow and Leeds over 16 years, were loved by British enthusiasts.

A vintage Spanish train: some of the coaches are fairly new (post 1920), but the overall appearance that of a long-distance train around 1910 complete with light 2-6-0 for light rail. The 57" drivers rarely took us above 40 mph

At Beniajan, just beyond Alqueiras, we wait in the siding for an Alicante-bound train led by an even rarer type of Mogul: 130/2083, one of six top heavy engines, this one built in 1910 by Henschel in Germany for the FC Medina del Campo a Salamanca. With 63" drivers, these were largely passenger engines.

Turning west into Andalucia, beyond Huercal — mountains closing in but a rich valley again. This ancient hill town along the Rio Almanzara may be Arboletas, 25 miles south of Almendricos

Another rare bird on the Alicante-Grenada line: at Murcia, the major city en route, we stop next to ex-Central of Aragon 0-6-6-0 #060-4006 (Henschel, 1927) waiting to follow us out to Alcantarilla on a very slow local to Albacete, on the Madrid line. The climb out of the huerta will need the mallet's power, and its 47" drivers.

With a fresh, and newer, loco to cope with grades the Correo climbs out of Baza for Zujar-Freila.

The stationmaster's rolled flag, the standard "home signal" on basic railways like Alicante-Granada, brings up the complex subject of Spanish signaling, which was still a mix of devices and practices dating from the 1860s to the 1950s. Traditional dispatching, inherited from the private companies, was timetable and train-order, using telegraph and later telephone for orders when extras ran or timetabled trains were late. At stations there were manually-controlled signals, usually a simple color-light but sometimes ancient semaphores or French-style disc-and-diamond.

In British terminology, these were usually "distant" signals, warning the engineer of the absolute "home" signal at the station. On the lines we rode, the home signal (at least in day time) was the red flag displayed by the stationmaster, furled tightly for "clear" and unfurled for "stop." This was true even on the heavily-traveled line from Castellón to Sagunto. On other lines the "home" signal would have been mechanical or color-light.

According to Trevor Rowe, about 570 miles were manual block single line, 82 miles manual block double, 1330 miles color-light home and starting signals, and 2700 miles of mechanical signals at stations with electric lights at night. As Rowe noted, the manual signaling was very much like British operation before about 1885, when signal boxes, telegraphs with elaborate bell-codes, and absolute-block working became required by law. At the other extreme, most important Spanish main lines by the mid-Sixties had automatic signalling–384 miles of automatic block and 810 miles of Centralized Traffic Control, the latter especially valuable since many trunk routes, including Madrid-Barcelona, were still largely single track.

After the relaxing stroll at Zujar, we toiled into the dusk at Guadix, on the Almeria line, for another engine change and the last lap over another summit into Granada. Beyond Guadix, junction for Almeria, we were back on the old Andaluces system. It was a long day, about 17 hours in an upholstered but bumpy 6-wheeled wooden coach; but it was our ultimate experience of traditional rail travel.

This historic route did enjoy a modest upgrade over the

next decade. By 1973 the Correo had been replaced by a through Barcelona- Granada train carrying couchettes and a snack lounge, cutting four hours with fewer stops. The old Automotor was now a new T.E.R., which saved only 40 minutes, suggesting that track remained traditional. As noted, the line from Almendricos to Guadix was torn up in the 1980s.

Granada, that mecca for English-speaking tourists since the early 19th Century, was for us a challenge. We couldn't ignore the Alhambra and Generalife, situated two miles from the RENFE station, but there were also two narrow-gauge electric lines out into the scenic mountains and fertile valleys south and east of the city. The more famous line was a 75cm route up into the Sierra Nevada mountains to the east, opened in 1925 to serve both mines and tourists. This scenic line climbed steeply along the Genil river through rocky gorges. It had been extended recently, and Rowe's <u>Railway Holiday</u> talked of a future aerial cableway from the new terminus at San Juan. This never happened, perhaps because the line was plagued by frequent rock falls, as on our visit when we could only reach a siding in the canyon, perhaps halfway up. This was far enough to serve picnickers.

Granada's 1920-style tramway fit into the traditional urban pattern.

The Granada city route approaching its terminal, near the Rio Genil at the Sierra Nevada station.

As (apparently) happened often, the Sierra Nevada was not running to its major stop, Maitena, due to washouts. So the motor runs around its trailers at the last siding below the blockage; most passengers then reboard for the inbound trip, while a few remain to picnic along Rio Genil.

Change for the Mediterranean: the Durcal line ran south about 18 miles, halfway to the ocean. The line's high point was this high bridge near Durcal. Many Spanish systems had one or two home-rebuilt "streamliners," usually dating from the austerity years around 1950

Ready for action: two rare 2-8-2Ts from the old Baza & Guadix Railway (on our previous route) prepare to storm the heavens up the grade with train 811, the 21.20 sleeping-car express to Madrid Atocha.

The other long ride our of Granada was much less-known, but equally fascinating. The Granada city tramway ran two long meter-gauge rural routes. one extending about 18 miles south, to the village of Durcal, halfway to the Mediterranean coast. At Durcal there had been a long aerial cableway to the little port of Motril, which carried general freight until abandoned. The Durcal line ran through rich farmland, with a spectacular high bridge near the terminus, where the hospitable crew arranged a photo for us.

The little Granada town tramway, and its two long extensions, seem to have opened in the mid-1920s, at about the same time as the Sierra Nevada. Gerald Brenan, in <u>South from Granada</u>, recalled trams only from the late 1920s:

The electric tram was in its first glory, sailing like a swan along the streets with far less creaking and shrieking than it makes today (1957), and throwing out their tentacles across fields and olive groves to the neighboring villages.

Granada's sprawling RENFE station was too big for its sparse train service. But it did boast the most spectacular sound of our journey, when two powerful 2-8-2 tank locos, of a small class built 1925-32, blasted up the hill and circled the city to head east for the junction at Moreda and on to the electrified main line at Linares. This was the 9.20 PM express, with sleepers and three classes of coach accommodation; an Almeria section was added at Moreda, the two running through to Madrid as a train separate from the other Andalucian services. The whole journey from Alicante was deep rural Spain and equally deep railway tradition.

CHAPTER IV

RAILS OF THE MESETA

Our overnight express from Granada and Almeria had taken a modern 3000 v. DC electric locomotive at Linares, since the busy, and in a few places single-track, Madrid-Cordoba line was the first long-distance route to be electrified throughout, rather than in suburban and mountainous fragments. As we came around the curve into the grand trainshed of Atocha Station, a mid-1950s English Electric loco was ready to leave with #402, the 8.30 AM Rapido to Seville and Malaga. A few tracks over was a heavy, stocky 4-8-2, built by Maquinista in 1948, ready to take out the 8.35 Rapido # 802 to Barcelona, taking 13 hours 25 minutes for the 420-odd miles to Barcelona Termino. (A tri-weekly Talgo made it in 9 hours 5 minutes). Old Atocha had a striking set of British-style semaphore signals, not really typical of Spain–if any particular style could be called typical. Those British signals were part of a local interlocking installed soon after the station opened in 1895.

Turning our attention to the rapidly-declining Madrid tramways, without much information, we found two semi-detached zones still run by trams, using modern Fiat streamliners, both double and single truck, rather like cars that ran in Rome and Turin for many years. Fiat had built a total of 160 "PCC's" for Madrid between 1942 and 1960; quite a number were streamlined single-truckers. These cars had transformed Madrid's streets from the 1940s scene eloquently evoked in Camillo José Cela's novel <u>The Hive</u>. Cela's cold, noisy, rickety trams, with fenders that street kids clung to, seemed remarkably like San Francisco's old Market Street Railway that I can recall from the same decade.

Atocha in transition: our overnighter from Granada and Almeria, Train 811, pulls into the grand shed at Madrid Atocha, on time at 8.25 AM. Next to our platform a diesel switcher is ready to pull out an earlier arrival, probably Train 885, the Correo from Barcelona which carried the Zaragoza sleepers. Next right is English Electric #7771, one of the last of 75 3000v. DC units built from 1952 to 1958. This leads Train 402, the 8.30 Rapido to Cordoba and Seville. A Barcelona express loads at far right.

The 8.30 to the south has departed, and tri-weekly Train 802, to Barcelona, begins to move behind one of the big modern 4-8-2s, class 241-2219 (La Maquinista, Barcelona, 1948), on time at 8.35.

These 4-8-2s were powerful locos, though reputedly not fleet-footed despite 69" drivers. Train 802 will take 13 hrs 25 mins for some 420 miles to Barcelona, compared to 10 hours 10 for the TAF and 9 hours 5 for the tri-weekly Talgo.

As another big modern engine waits below the British-style semaphores, another of the Primo de Rivera era locos, 242/0286, one of sixty 4-8-4Ts (Maquinista, 1924-27) comes in with a local train, probably from Getafe on the line to Extremadura.

Before traffic dominated Madrid: a Fiat streamliner has passed the Museo del Prado and now passes the 18th Century Cibeles Fountain in the Plaza of the same name (also known as Canovas del Castillo.)

On the south side: a few blocks south of the Delicias station, and perhaps ten blocks below Atocha, a Madrid Fiat on Route 37, from Atocha to the inner suburb of Usera, just across the Manzares river.

Three generations: the single-trucker tram near Cuatros Caminos, northwest of the centre, may be newer than the bus.

A newish line in a new development north of Madrid's Ciudad Universitaria. Policy had clearly changed, since new routes like this soon vanished. This urban-fringe area had seen bitter fighting in 1936, as local militias fought Franco's African troops.

There may still have been a tramway connection through the center; we saw trams heading up the Calle de Arocha from the station towards the center and amid already-burgeoning motor traffic along the Paseo del Prado, which by 2000 had turned into a truly hellish trafficway, capped by its own ceiling of smog. The two zones where we found the snazzy, smooth-sided Fiats were south of Atocha climbing into a 20th Century quarter, and in the University City and the hills beyond, to the northwest of Cuatros Caminos metro station, where single-truck streamliners ran out into a hilly middle-class neighborhood still under construction. The policy had clearly reversed under the policy of Franco's new economic ministers after 1957. Madrid was emulating prewar Paris, in deciding that traffic should and would grow, so a city must build underground Metros and motorways. Madrid had had 35 tram routes in the 1940s, reduced to seven in the mid-1960s, still clean and well-maintained. The last lines closed in 1972.

Other targets beckoned, and we saw no more. Our immediate targets were mixtures of history, architecture, and rail interest. In 1963 there was no Chamartin main-line station, or connecting main-line subway through the center to Atocha. Trains for the north and northwest left from the old Norte (Pio Principe) station, west of downtown behind the Royal Palace. Here departed through trains for seven major destinations, plus a moderate suburban service run with boxy EMUS build in the 1940s, when the long-delayed electrification to Avila and Segovia was finally completed.

Our first target was Philip II's vast palace at El Escorial, a "glowering barrack-like block" to Ray Alan in <u>Spanish Quest</u>, located, one suspects, for its relative inaccessibility far enough from Madrid to deter all but the most determined visitors to that busy royal recluse. At the station, I managed to record one of the 1940s Swiss locos that hauled the through expresses up the long grade to the Meseta at Avila.

The Meseta itself needs discussion, since it covers most of Spain, and from 1492 to 1975 its people usually ruled, and defined Spanish identity and values. Divided by mountains from the coastal areas to the East, North, and South, the meseta is undulating and crossed by mountain ranges, generating a sense of both beauty and monotony. Large areas were deforested a thousand years back, and parts denuded of topsoil by heavy sheep-grazing to create the parched La Mancha of Cervantes *Don Quixote*, the classic satire on the values of the Castilian elite. But most is arable, raising wheat and livestock. Elevations vary; Madrid, around 2000 feet above sea level, is Europe's highest capital; Avila up in the central Sierra de Gredos around 3700; León at the northern edge of the Meseta lies at 2625. To the north, the long, high, rugged Cantabrian ranges divide the dry plain of Castilla y León from the rain-soaked "green Spain" of Asturias, Cantabria and the Basque provinces. This great central tableland was traditional Spain, which controlled the Peninsula and ruled the Spanish Empire for 350 years, and was the centre of the traditionalist revolt against modern Republican Spain in 1936. In 1963, still, manners were different here stiffer, cooler; less "Latin," though grave and polite. A striking trait of the Meseta was the beauty and penetrating clarity of the spoken language there, whose sheer force and gravity seemed to generate comprehension. Much of the energy of Spanish politics at least down to the 1980s came from the conflict between the austere, bureaucratic Mesetans and the more liberal, more entrepreneurial peoples of the usually-wealthier peripheries, the "golden fringe.".

Our electric local on to Avila took about 75 minutes for the 43 miles. The station and yards at Avila were not especially busy for most of the midday hours, and we took the 15 minute-walk to the grand old walled town, with its cathedral incorporated into the defenses and views of the rolling tableland around the city as yet unpolluted by suburban dreck. (Which, one acknowledges, was a reflection of high-perched Avila's stagnation since the days of St. Teresa).

Back at the often-peaceful station, we were able to record another of those ever-present Victorian teakettles. This one was 98 years old, one of the first 0-8-0s built for the Norte by Cail in France in 1865. The star attractions, though, were two of Avila's most famous living residents, the ten almost-new 4-8-4s in unique green livery, that were assigned largely to a single duty, hauling heavy expresses over the unelectrified central section of the former Norte main line to Valladolid and the North. The daytime Iberia Express often drew a 242/2001, but their major service was on the heaviest of the parade of overnight trains that came up the hill from Madrid between 11 PM and 2 AM.

The 242/2001s, built by Maquinista in 1955-56, were not quite RENFE's heaviest–there was a group of giant 2-10-2s used for coal trains–but they came very close: total weight 212,700kgs. with 70½" drivers. By comparison, the standard modern 2-8-2s weighed 166,000 kg and had 61" drivers. From the platform I captured the 242's best angle–from the front, they looked rather squat.

Alas, even in 1963 we were not enthusiastic enough to camp out overnight on the Avila platform, so I can only try to reconstruct the midnight drama from a crumbling *Guia General de Ferrocarriles*. A few of the services to the north (to Santander) used the single-track line via Segovia. All the rest–to Galicia via Zamora, to Palencia, León and Oviedo/Gijon, to Bilbao and to the French border at Irun/Hendaye–ran via Avila, and all had one or more overnight trains. The busiest route, to Miranda for Bilbao or the border, had four overnights, three with Wagons-lits. These were the likeliest to draw the 242 class. Overall, some six expresses departed Avila northwards in 90 minutes, from 23.59 (Gijon) to 01.29 (Galicia). Most took just 8 minutes to change from electric to steam power. This grand steam finale lasted another five years, until RENFE finally closed the electrification gap; it was memorialized by David P. Morgan in a *Trains* piece, "The Green 4-8-4s of Avila."

1940s electric stock at El Escorial: 1500-volt MUs at the station on a local to Madrid, and Swiss-built 7510 of 1944 coming in with a train for Avila, and probably beyond. The steeply-graded Madrid-Avila line was planned for electrification by 1930, but only finished in 1946.

Deepest Spain: the Meseta from Avila with the 11th Century walls in foreground.

Almost as old as the walls: ancient 0-6-0s and 0-8-0s were routine sights, simmering quietly at Spanish stations. But, befitting Avila, its station pilot was one of the oldest, the 040/2001 series built in 1865 by Cail in France for the Ciudad Rodrigo-Badajoz Railway near the Portuguese border

Avila's star attraction in 1963, one of the ten seven-year-old 4-8-4s which worked heavy express passenger trains over the non-electrified centre section of the Norte main line between Avila and Miranda de Ebro.

Local passenger trains on the non-electrified main line from León towards Madrid were run by these older, lighter but powerful French-designed compound 4-8-0s. The design dated to 1912, though 240/4045, the last of the class, was built by Henschel in 1921

Tradition and modernity at León: a compound 4-8-0 of 1921 with a local passenger from Palencia, and a new British-built electric of the 7700 class on a freight for the West.

After Avila our next glimpse of the Meseta was at León, about 180 miles north-west on the plain leading up to the Cantabrian mountains. León is a magical little city with splendid architecture capped by a spectacular Gothic cathedral that contains the largest and most brilliant expanse of stained glass in Iberia if not the world. Its iron RENFE trainshed was not very busy, but had interest as an engine-changing point between steam and electric. In a familiar Spanish pattern, the electrification was away from Madrid, where heavy freight and mountain grades dictated prudent expenditure. The Pajares Pass north to Oviedo and Gijon was electrified throughout by the mid-Fifties, and operated with streamlined 3000-volt English Electric engines. The line west to Galicia, also steeply-graded and a heavy coal line, was electrified beginning in the mid-fifties.

Chapter V

RAILS OF INDUSTRY: THE NARROW GAUGES OF COAST AND CORDILLERA

There was a second station in León, up west of the Cathedral, built in the 1920s in the "señorial" (neo-traditional) style. This was the passenger terminus of Spain's largest and busiest meter-gauge line under one ownership, the Ferrocarril La Robla, known locally as El Hullero, the coal-miner, for its endless flow of coaltrains from mines along the southern slope of the Cantabrian mountains to the iron and steel works around Bilbao, some 225 miles northeast of León. With the expansion of domestic coal-mining a part of Spain's drive for self-sufficiency in the 1940s and 50s, the FCLR had bought meter-gauge locos second-hand from Spanish and foreign systems, including Tunisia and the Rhaetian Railway in Switzerland. It also had sixteen 2-8-0s built by Baldwin around 1900.

La Robla had opened in the 1890s, but the passenger-oriented branch down to León not until after 1920. So we saw few of El Hullero's 74-odd steam locos and none of its Beyer-Garratts; but we did capture the magic moment when one of the handsome Tunisian Pacifics, built in 1913 for that French colony, charged out of León's quiet depot with the 17.50 train to Guardo. In all, León La Robla hosted four shorter-distance locals plus the through Correo to Bilbao Concordia, which in true American style paused for lunch at the midpoint of Mataporquera.

The FC La Robla played a significant role in Spain's railway development. The line's chief engineer in the 1920s and 30s, Alejandro Goicoechea Omar, developed the Talgo lightweight-articulated principle, at first for coal cars. Finding little interest on that freight-hauler in applying the principle to passenger trains, he left to promote it for high-speed passenger service, and in the 1940s found converts in the new RENFE management, who saw it as a relatively economical way to run faster trains over light and deteriorated track. The early Talgos were few in number, and usually gave a disconcerting bang-bang ride on jointed rail (as I recall vividly from Boston & Maine's Reading line). In 1963 there were only a couple of Talgo services, but a large tranche of improved Talgos came in the mid-1960s. With better rail being laid, these began to cut times over more lines, without the discomfort of the pioneers. And the 1960s Talgos lasted into the 21st Century; we rode one from Madrid to Bilbao in 2000, and found it a little shabby but comfortable. Indeed, the hugely-overpowered ride from Miranda de Ebro over the hill to Bilbao behind a huge Japanese-design electric was quite thrilling, with acceleration worthy of a hot-rod American interurban like the North Shore line.

Meter-gauge tradition in old Léon: Linke-Hoffman 2-6-2T of 1923, named Conde de Vildosola after one of the FC La Robla's backers, does some evening switching at the compact Léon terminus.

The FC La Robla's last steam locos were five 4-6-2s bought second-hand from Tunisia to speed up the single through passenger train of the day, which even with the Pacifics took 11 hrs 22 mins for about 215 miles (including a lunch stop in Mataporquera). Here #185, built at Belfort by Societé Alsacienne in 1928 to a 1914 design, departs for Guardo with the 17.50 local.

The Tunisian Pacific charges out of Léon with train 11, the 17.50 to Guardo, carrying 1st and 3rd class coaches. These were FCLR's most admired locos, but there were seven other wheel arrangements, including Garratts, and Baldwin 2-8-0s, among the 74 engines.

Industrial North: characteristic weather at Mieres, about twelve miles south of Oviedo, the pioneer steelworks of this mountainous industrial zone. The Fabrica de Mieres had several private lines, standard and narrow gauge. The standard-gauge 0-6-0 is on lease from RENFE; it had run main-line service on the Pajares Pass from the early 1880s until electrification in the 1920s

We did not travel on La Robla's through Correo since other rails beckoned directly north. The 110-mile Pajares Pass line through the Cordillera Cantabrica to the industrial zone around Oviedo and Gijon is one of the great scenic lines of Iberia, with long 2% grades and numerous reverse curves on the north side of the pass, up one side of a canyon, then the other. It had to rise some 2800 feet in 13 miles as the crow flies. A rack line was considered, but the long, twisting route up to Pajares Tunnel, kept to a steady 2%, finally opened in 1884. Because of heavy coal traffic, this was a major route from opening day, and the big 0-6-0s and 0-8-0s labored slowly, taking 4½ hours for 33 miles, including many stops for water and passing other trains. With the filthy conditions for passengers in numerous tunnels, a demand for electrification came early, and in 1925 the central section, Ujo to Busdongo, opened with a dozen General Electric locos (the Swiss charged too much). As noted, electrification of the whole line, with new British locos, opened in 1955.

After an enjoyable ride up the sunny south slope, we soon discovered why Asturias is known as "Green Spain." It rains, and rains some more; we had a misty descent of what did appear a very Swiss, if heavily shrouded, landscape. Down the hill, around Ujo, we began to encounter the dense zone of mines and ironworks that Mike Bent has described superbly in <u>Narrow Gauge Rails Through the Cordillera</u>. We were lucky enough to stop next to the veteran steelworks at Mieres, where a row of Victorian locos were lined up, including one of the Norte's original 0-6-0s, named after Asturian worthies, that had run the hill line from 1884 to 1925.

Beyond Oviedo, we spent a very long, rain-soaked day traversing the three connected meter-gauge lines along (though rarely in sight of) the Bay of Biscay, to Santander and then (after dark) to the Art-Nouveau Concordia station in Bilbao. There are few good pictures from this journey: weather was bad, we were tired, and the Civil Guards, in this traditional zone of unrest, less tolerant than usual. After years of repression and quiet, strike action had recently reappeared in Asturias. I did record the narrow/standard gauge crossing of the isolated, British- owned

FC Langreo at El Berrón, just east of Oviedo. It is pleasant to note that almost all of this great narrow-gauge empire has survived into the 21st Century, with considerable suburban electrification around Oviedo and Santander, and new freight flows, especially from the remains of the steel industry. Mike Bent wrote an excellent survey of the situation in FEVE in Today's Railways for March, 2005. By far the most vivid picture remaining is one existing in memory only–our arrival in Bilbao, far after dark: a vision of a Victorian city at night, like an engraving by Gustav Doré–sheets of rain, blurring the city's lights; steam everywhere from locomotives, factories, boats on the river at our feet. I don't know how accurate a picture of Bilbao in 1963 this is–did steamboats come so far up the Nervión? but it is firmly fixed in that creative mental power called Memory.

Pioneer power: Jovellanos (named for an Asturian reformer of the 1700s) was the proud name on 030/2414, one of 38 engines built in Germany in 1881-2, with 54" drivers for the opening of the steeply-graded Asturias-Galicia-León Railway over the Pajores Pass.

Where standard was narrow: a train on the British-built, 4'8 1/2" gauge Langreo Railway waits at the crossing of the meter-gauge Economicos de Asturias for the morning Correo from Oviedo to Santander to clear El Berrón before it continues south to the industrial areas. #34 was an 0-6-0T probably built in the U.S. around 1930; the 0-6-0T at right was from the Dutch State Railway, bought in 1954.

The North Coast network in busy days: of Llanes our Correo was on the Ferrocarril Cantabrico, and we've taken siding near Rudaguera for the tri-weekly Automotor train

Along the Cantabrian coast on the FC Cantabrico. Most of the long meter-gauge network is somewhat inland. It still runs in the 21st Century, with a very sparse passenger service except around the cities, and with some traffic between facilities of the struggling steel industry, attempting to survive after Spain's opening to the world threatened traditional industries.

EPILOGUE 2006

Most of the trains illustrated here vanished fairly soon after our trip–all the tramways (except the tiny Tranvia Blau in Barcelona) within a decade. The smaller, lighter narrow-gauge lines closed as roads improved and government policy became more impatient with them. But there are three grand survivors. Almost all of the North Coast meter-gauge system survives, now under FEVE control. La Robla lost most of its coal business as the Basque steel industry declined due to foreign competition, but lurched along for decades due to a power plant built along the line. It has now been upgraded, its through passenger train restored by the regional government as a tourist attraction, and a seasonal, luxury Transcantabrico running León-Bilbao-Oviedo-Ferrol. The last section opened after 1963, against outside advice, because General and Senora Franco had ties at both ends. Other narrow- gauge survivors are the Catalan system out of Barcelona, and the scenic Alicante-Denia.

RENFE electrified slowly, dieselized more rapidly–though some steam lingered in Galicia until the mid-70s. Many steam locos were preserved, and a few now run on excursions from Madrid, Lleida, and occasionally Ourense. As of 1990 RENFE was losing longer-distance passenger business; a respected British magazine said the long-distance services were in their final phase. But the huge success of the Madrid-Seville AVE line, opened in 1992, changed official attitudes, leading to an extensive high-speed program, still only partly carried out. The second major AVE line, Madrid-Barcelona, is open from Madrid to Zaragoza and Lleida, with construction proceeding to Barcelona and the French border, to complete a Paris-Barcelona-Madrid TGV/AVE link by about 2011. Within Spain, the extensive planned network has been scaled back as costs rise. Still, a new Madrid-Medina del Campo cutoff will make the routes to North and Northwest more competitive. And major new lines from Madrid to Valencia, Alicante and Cartegena seem certain, with a long high-speed cutoff to Galicia also planned.

The relatively flat Barcelona-Valencia route is already upgraded, with hourly 125 mph Euromed trains. One casualty seems to be the new line replacing the abandoned Alicante-Granada line, RENFE's only complete closure of a through route. All in all, it is still an ambitious program to ensure that rail remains a major force in the life of the vibrant, confident Spain of the 21st Century.